Stuart Wilson

CW00835661

THE CANCER POEMS

Stuart Wilson

Stuart Wilson

Stuart Wilson

Stuart Wilson

THE CANCER POEMS

On the 5th June 2012 my wife Angie was diagnosed with breast cancer.

These poems were written during her long period of treatment.

This book is dedicated to her and to our families, friends, neighbours and local community for their love, kindness and support.

I hope these poems go some way at least to express the love and admiration I have for her.

Stuart Wilson
Crete, 2014

Stuart Wilson

For those that survived
and for those that did not.

And for their families and friends
who shared in their suffering.

Stuart Wilson

Stuart Wilson

I AM NOT A DOCTOR OR A SURGEON, I AM A HUSBAND

I love my wife more than all there is
 but that did not prevent her from becoming unwell.
Love is a balm, a salve
love in itself can not remove something
so devious so wicked as this.

Love can support, embolden,
comfort and reassure.
Metaphorically it can mend a broken heart
but it cannot remove a tumour or repair damaged tissue
or make blood run true.

I could not love you more
though apart from giving support
and reassurances I could do little.
Bolster your confidence
when I could
remind you often how wonderful
how beautiful and feminine you are
apply love's balm and touch you with it's salve.

I am not a doctor or a surgeon
I am a husband
A man that loves his wife
more than all there is
That is my occupation, my job
The thing I am most concerned with.
Something that now more than ever
for you and for us
I need to do well.

ASSURANCES

Everything has a time
and a place, conversations,
questions, assurances.
All valid if timed well
The morning of major surgery
is not such a time.

'You will wake up won't you?'
were the words I foolishly asked.
'You won't leave?'
In my head the words were formed another way.
This may be the last time I see you
were repeating over and over and over.

What if you don't wake up
sometimes people don't.
You are a person, therefore
that qualifies you
in my mind at that moment
you were fully qualified.

You could not give assurances
other than to say you would not leave me
and I had no right
to ask them of you.
After the operation you spoke.
'I told you I would wake up'
were the first words you said.
'I told you I would wake up'.

My girl, my girl
You little rascal.

Stuart Wilson

Stuart Wilson

CORRIDORS

Today it is ultrasound, undertaken
every six weeks between tests and treatments.
CAT scans, bloods taken,
Intravenous Herceptin to starve your cancer,
administered every twenty one days.
It will be fifteen months
before this treatment is finished.
Tamoxifen to stop your hormones from raging
and creating a new cancer
enlisting its help to prevent a return.

You are in the treatment room
and I am in the corridor.
White, clinical, impersonal
the same as any hospital corridor
in any country.

Maria attends to you
kindly empathetic thorough Maria
Professional too
I would take that quality above the others
for now.
We trust Maria.

The corridor echoes
as hospital corridors do
a bench to sit on
your treatment room beside it.
The door closed,
More probing for you.

I hope when you leave the room
you will be smiling
a message you transmit to me
a statement that all is well
for this time.

Stuart Wilson

Clear the door, soon, walk towards me
and show me your smile.
You know how I love your smile.
There was a time when
I thought I might lose it.

People walk the corridor
This way and that
trying to find their way around
or standing staring out of the windows.
Awaiting news of their own.
Some lost in the vastness of the hospital.
Others lost in another way.
Sitting waiting or pacing
What else is there to do?

The examination over
I hear you preparing to leave the room
Thanking Maria,
your voice friendly but flat
business like.
I try not to read too much
into the tone, I would only
imagine the worst.

Go on smile at me
Go ahead and show it to me.
You never lost it
Even during the worst days.
It never left you for long.
Walk towards me,
 send out your message.
I'm longing to see it.
And you know how I love your smile.

Stuart Wilson

HAIR LOSS

Quite soon, along with the vomiting,
 the soaring temperature and the screaming bones
hair loss began.

Large clumps would appear on your pillow
attaching themselves to your perspiring face
as you attempted sleep.

Thin strands of hair would fall into your eyes
while you washed, tried to read,
or cook when you were able.
And when the sight or smell of food being prepared
did not encourage nausea.

Eyebrows too and eyelashes were affected.
The hair on your legs and arms gone
soon all evidence of hair
would be removed from your body,
as though it had never existed in the first place.
Like a new born child pale and smooth
and not of this world.

You who would shave under your arms daily,
and apply cream above your lip
as a regular bathroom ritual.
You would have no need now
for the razor or the creams.
One day you hoped they would be removed
from their place at the back of the cabinet,
if you responded well to treatment
and the cancer has not travelled
has not changed, mutated or grown.

Stuart Wilson

In an effort to gain control,
take ownership you said
you chose to cut your hair short,
make it your decision this lack of hair
and for a time, a short time
it was better for you.

Then more was gone so that
bare patches of skin appeared
where your lovely hair had been.

You shaved your head, make it your decision,
having no hair
and you took to wearing head scarves
to maintain your femininity and
to retain a semblance of control
regarding your appearance
and to off set questions.

In addition you were told
the chemotherapy would affect
the nails on your fingers
and on your toes
and that you may lose these also.
And teeth there was often a problem with teeth
We hoped you would be spared that at least.
We wished you had been spared it all.

If these were just the external manifestations
of your treatment.
No wonder then you felt
as though a fire raged within you.

Stuart Wilson

Stuart Wilson

Well then! Fall out if you must
Nails too if that is to be the way.
Let the therapy do its worst
but let it perform its job also.
Make her well, make the suffering
and the loss mean something.
She only has so much courage
please don't escalate things any more.
Let it be worthwhile, all of this,
make the chemotherapy justify its position
make her well.

But I know you miss it your hair
what woman wouldn't,
occasionally changing the colour,
trying different styles to match your mood
to compliment an outfit
or just to change things.

You will always be beautiful to me
and your dignity is still intact.
Such a thing as hair loss even in these circumstances
could not change that.
So defined your dignity
it has never left you
not even for a moment
nothing could ever deprive you of that.

So, for now you experiment with head scarves
different colours, different styles.
I know it is not the same
how could it be.
Forever changed now
but your hair will grow back,
slowly to begin with
and you will style it again.
Your nails will grow strong
and the colour return to your skin.

Stuart Wilson

When you are well,
when you are well again.

Stuart Wilson

ROAD TRIP

Mile after mile, kilometre
upon kilometre the road rolls by
"There are the mountains that look
like Snowdonia or the Alps" we say.
The chalky houses of Rethymno
The road works now. Then the
goats that are always in the road
around this bend which houses
a fearful bump.

The view of the sea
like Scotland or Cornwall,
We don't know we are just talking.
The rocks from this aspect or that
all angles beautiful, but
our comments a little worn now
After 38 trips.

El Grecos village we pass
and make comment upon.
Perhaps one day we will spend the night there
Without hospitals or worry
And without fear.

You in your seat
which has become a study
a studio, a dining room.
A room for knitting
-I'm sorry I don't know what
that would be called -
a kitchen and at times a bed
only occasionally a bed
- so tough for someone so beautiful -

Stuart Wilson

Still you, there in your seat,
15,000 kilometres and never a complaint,
just a smile and a confirmation
"I will be well".

To the hospital and every time
 you had to go.
There was no other way.
I would have gone in your place
taken the treatment for you
the cancer too we know.
I tried to ease your pain and
emulate your courage, impossible to do

You made friends with your doctors and the nurses
Getting to know them, trusting them
admiring what they do
and the spirit in which they do it.
And I knowing more of you myself
admiring you more, even more
and loving you.
Through all of this the pain the fear and the bravery
who would not admire you.
And who could fail to love you.

Stuart Wilson

RUN

You know life is a serious business
still though I would like to dig a hole.
We could hide in it
pretend that we are invisible
pretend the world had gone away
no one would ever know
and we would not tell them.

We could run away,
catch a train to London
or a bus to the seaside,
paddle in the waves
eat fish and chips.
Make believe you are twenty again,
make believe nothing is wrong.

I know that we cannot
we must stay
visit hospitals, work hard
work tirelessly to make you well.

We will not run
you must stay
and I will not run without you.
There is no choice.
You will visit the hospital
and take your medication
and do what the doctors tell you to do.

One day though you will take off the scarves
and your breathing will return.
That time will come, really.
One day life will not be such a serious business for you.
We will catch that bus to the coast
eat chips on the beach,
act the goat in the sea.

Stuart Wilson

Rejoice in your health
and reclaim our lives and
run because you choose to run
because you want to run
because you can.

Stuart Wilson

GOOD DOCTORS

Can you not leave the girl alone?
She has suffered so much.
I know that you cannot
your aim is to get her well
and we are grateful for that.

But the cutting and the scars,
the sickness, the vomiting,
the scorched skin, the stitches,
the hair loss, the chemicals
the needles, the therapy and the bloods,
please leave her alone soon.

The girl has done enough
though she would do more I know.
But you should know doctors
how great you have been, how brilliant.
To leave her in health,
to make her well.
She loves life and would like it
to continue
and that is all she would ask of herself.

And from you good doctors
with your skills and your kindness
she could ask no more
already she knows your worth
and for as long as we live
we owe you our gratitude
and we owe you our lives.

MAKE THEM WAIT

I am frightened of this other world quality I see in you.
Not from this place, not from here.
I have always believed that
but not like this.
Your spirits are good, I know
though your eyes are dark.
Your skin stretched and taut and grey
The colour of a winter sky
No longer the colour that skin should be.

And when you say goodnight to me
your simple 'I'm going to sleep now' takes on a different meaning.
I wonder for a moment
 if, you are preparing me, warning me.
Putting things in their place,
while knowing that I would need longer than we have,
to ever be prepared.

The love within you would attempt
to negate the fear,
as the angel in you would
try to ease me.
I could never be ready my love
not in a thousand years.
I could never be prepared.

Don't join them please,
your fellow angels, not yet.
Don't answer their call,
make them wait a while.
Can't they wait?
Tell them you have work still to do here.

Stuart Wilson

Fabricate if you must, though Angels would know a lie I think.
Tell them there are people who love you
people who need you
and would not survive if you were to leave.
Tell them anything,
beg on my behalf if need be,
they are Angels they will understand.

Lie, convince them, plead,
tell them anything but don't go.
Tell them you cannot go,
make them wait a while.
Become deaf to their calling
say that you are not ready.
Let them take me instead
I am prepared, I am ready.

Say anything you must
but make them listen to you
Make them wait, please,
Make them wait.

Stuart Wilson

<u>SCARS</u>

Your scars are not beautiful
scars are not made this way.
They are not ugly or unattractive either.
A part of you now, evidence of all you have undergone.
Not unattractive heartbreaking though
heartbreaking the thing that happened to you.

Your surgeon was kind and careful with her knife
and exacting in her calculations,
mindful of taking enough from you
to remove all of the damaged tissue
and excise from your breast the tumour too.
Aware of taking no more than was necessary
understanding the importance of this
to you, the importance of this
to any woman.

A physical reminder, yet
there is no need for that,
we remember well enough.
These scars will fade
you have been told,
though never leaving you completely.
We understand that
and will remain watchful.
And you will continue to be well
and more special than you have ever been.

I am not alone in this thinking.

Stuart Wilson

<u>YOU</u>

And we, you and I
will never have this time again
As bad as it was we faced it
resisted and challenged it together.
Time spent with you
this time this terrible time.

Difficult year,
beautiful, beautiful you.

Stuart Wilson

THE GIRL THAT WAS SO UNWELL

A stain across you now,
a label attached,
a badge of honour some have said.
Kind people, meaning well,
only well.
Marked though, a stamp,
an imprint, a title,
'A Cancer Survivor'.
The girl that was so unwell.

Stuart Wilson

Stuart Wilson

<u>THERE WILL BE NO FUNERAL</u>

And so there will be no funeral,
the final scan is clear.
No coffin or ground dug
fresh and deep, not now.
Those solemn thoughts we both harboured
can rest, can wait.
There will be no funeral.

Purged from your body
that thing that threatened your life.
It is clear!
Gone from your breast
It is clear!
The scan is clear.
We want to shout it
The scan is clear!
It is gone.

One day a parting will come
we understand the terms of this agreement.
The print written between the lines
of the contract that is a marriage.
A life shared,
eventually a death too.

One day we will have no choice
but to face that.
Not now though,
that day is not this day.
Today is for looking ahead
and for looking back,
but not too much
this day is for this moment.

There will be tears, I know,
and laughter also.

Stuart Wilson

After all you have been through
the pain and fear you have endured
you have earned your tears.

Today is for you,
today is for us
the undisciplined ruffian
the cunning thug
has been shown the door.

There is nothing for him here.

Stuart Wilson

Stuart Wilson

DANCE, DANCE ,DANCE

And you dancing at a Greek wedding
arms entwined, feet moving in time.
You that could not walk to the shops
without looking for a bench to sit on
or a post to lean against
until breathlessness had left you.

Dancing at a wedding,
your rhythm good and your breathing too.
There was a time when I thought
you would never dance again.
There was a time I was convinced
I would lose you.

You proved me wrong
go on continue to prove me wrong
dance now and show me
the error of my thinking.
What a fool I was to doubt you
carry on make me look foolish
I am all for it.

I had not considered your will,
the strength of it
the strength contained within you.
I had not acknowledged your ability to bend,
or your refusal to drop.

Dance for a hundred years
then maybe more one thousand, keep going,
to dance is to rejoice, to celebrate
and we have much to celebrate
so much.

Stuart Wilson

Dance,
you are the best I have ever seen,
the best dancer in the world
dance, dance, dance.
I have never seen anything this beautiful,
I have never seen anything so lovely.

Stuart Wilson

Stuart Wilson

THE GIRL WHO IS WELL NOW

'We won't need to see you for three months'
The doctor is kind but
matter of fact when he says this.
It is not new to him,
He is a doctor, an oncologist,
he has said these words before
but not to you.
In eighteen months
you have never heard these words.

Beautiful words,
 at this time the most beautiful words
the world has ever known.
Intoxicating, magical,
reassuring, liberating, poetic
perhaps most of all liberating
free from the weekly tyranny of needles
and fluids dripped into your veins.
Free too, for three months from fear.

Well enough now not to ask
for an appointment paper for the next visit.
Healthy enough that there will be
no tubes inserted into tired, diminished veins.
No blood taken,
or tumour markers looked for.
For three months, three months.

The girl that was so unwell
has a new stamp now.
A different label,
a new title.
One that you wear far better
and one that becomes you entirely.
The girl that was so brave,
the girl that is well now.

Stuart Wilson

Stuart Wilson

A CHRISTMAS THANK YOU TO ANGIE WILSON 2013

Angie, thank you for getting well
I was not always convinced it could be done.
And you never had a doubt.
Thank you for your conviction
you were right, you were strong, you were brave.
I've never doubted you before
I promise you it won't happen again.

Thank you for the warmth
that flows within you.
Even in the hardest times.
Thank you also for the light
that shines from you.
When all the world is
bathed in darkness.

And thank you my Angie
for this year, I would have
spent it with no other
I spent it with you
I consider my self blessed for that.

And thank you too for
showing me something new of yourself
Your humility, the patience you possess, and
the modesty regarding your courage.
Thank you too for showing
your appreciation for the doctors
And for the staff for the things that they do
And the manner in which they do them.

Stuart Wilson

Thank you for letting me help you,
for keeping me in,
for allowing me to worry
To watch over you,
For taking your arm when you crossed the road,
for bringing you tea in the morning
for allowing me to love you,
Thank you.

Thank you for sharing yourself with me.
What a wonderful wife you are,
What a lucky man am I.
Thank you for your love
a gift beyond all calculation,
And thank you Angie, my Angie
for getting well, for saying that you would
and keeping your promise,
Thank you.

Printed in Great Britain
by Amazon.co.uk, Ltd.,
Marston Gate.